ESMERALDA

---

by

VICTOR HUGO

British Library Cataloguing-in-Publication Data
A catalogue record for this book is available from
the British Library

CONTENTS

Victor Hugo 5

ESMERALDA 11

ACT I 13

ACT II 30

ACT III 43

ACT IV 56

VICTOR HUGO

Victor Marie Hugo was born on 26th February 1802, in Besançon, Franche-Comté, France. He was a political campaigner, artist, poet, novelist and dramatist of the Romantic movement, considered one of the greatest French writers of all time.

Hugo's father was a freethinking republican who considered Napoléon a hero, and his mother was a Catholic Royalist, who was executed in 1812 for plotting against the legendary general. Hugo's childhood was a period of national political turmoil. Napoléon was proclaimed Emperor two years after Hugo's birth, and the Bourbon Monarchy was restored before his eighteenth birthday. The opposing political and religious views of Hugo's parents reflected the forces that would battle for supremacy in France throughout his life.

As a young man, his mother dominated his education and upbringing, and as a result Hugo's early work in poetry and fiction reflects her passionate devotion to both King and Faith. It was only later, during the events leading up to France's 1848 Revolution, that he would begin to rebel against his Catholic Royalist education and instead champion Republicanism and Freethought. Hugo was also a rebellious young man, and on falling in love with his childhood friend Adèle Foucher (1803–

1868), became secretly engaged against his mothers wishes. Because of his close relationship with his mother, Hugo waited until after his mother's death (in 1821) to marry Adèle in 1822.

Hugo published his first novel the year following his marriage (*Han d'Islande*, 1823), and his second three years later (*Bug-Jargal*, 1826). Between 1829 and 1840 he would publish five more volumes of poetry, cementing his reputation as one of the greatest elegiac and lyric poets of his time. Victor Hugo's first mature work of fiction appeared in 1829, and reflected the acute social conscience that would infuse his later work. *The Last Day of a Condemned Man* would have a profound influence on later writers such as Albert Camus, Charles Dickens, and Fyodor Dostoevsky. It was soon followed by *The Hunchback of Notre-Dame* (in 1831), which was quickly translated into other language across Europe.

Adèle and Victor Hugo had their first child, Léopold, in 1823, but the boy died in infancy. The following year, on 28th August 1824, the couple's second child, Léopoldine was born, followed by Charles in 1826, François-Victor in 1828, and Adèle in 1830. Hugo's oldest and favourite daughter, Léopoldine, died at the age of nineteen in 1843, shortly after her marriage to Charles Vacquerie. On 4th September 1843, she drowned in the Seine at Villequier, pulled down by her heavy skirts, when a boat overturned. Her young husband also died trying to save her. The death left her father devastated; Hugo was travelling with his mistress at the time in the south of France, and first learned about Léopoldine's death from a newspaper he read in a cafe.

Hugo wrote many poems about his daughter's tragic life and death, and many biographers have claimed that he never completely recovered from this traumatic incident. His most famous poem is probably *Demain, Dès L'aube,* in which he describes visiting her grave. He began planning a major novel about social misery and injustice as early as the 1830s, but it would take a full seventeen years for *Les Misérables* to be realized and finally published in 1862. On its publication, the critical establishment was generally hostile to the novel, with Gustave Flaubert claiming he found within it 'neither truth nor greatness' and Baudelaire castigating it as 'tasteless and inept.' Despite this, *Les Misérables* was a massive hit with the public, and today remains Victor Hugo's most enduringly popular work.

After three unsuccessful attempts, Hugo was finally elected to the Académie Française in 1841, solidifying his position in the world of French arts and letters. He was also elevated to the peerage by King Louis-Philippe in the same year and entered the Higher Chamber as a *pair de France*, where he spoke against the death penalty and social injustice, and in favour of freedom of the press and self-government for Poland. In 1848, Hugo was elected to the Parliament as a conservative. In 1849 he broke with the conservatives when he gave a noted speech calling for the end of misery and poverty. When Louis Napoleon (Napoleon III) seized complete power in 1851, establishing an anti-parliamentary constitution, Hugo openly declared him a traitor to France.

Hugo decided to live in exile after Napoleon III's coup d'état at the end of 1851. After leaving France, he lived in Brussels briefly in 1851, before moving to the Channel Islands, first to Jersey (1852–1855) and then to the smaller island of Guernsey in 1855, where he stayed until 1870. Whilst in exile, Hugo published his famous political pamphlets against Napoleon

III, *Napoléon le Petit* and *Histoire d'un Crime,* which whilst banned in France, had a strong impact. Although Napoleon III proclaimed a general amnesty in 1859, the author stayed in exile, only returning when Napoleon was forced from power in 1870. Hugo's next novel, *Troilers of the Sea* turned away from the social and political themes so prevalent in *Les Miserables.* It told the story of a man hoping to gain the approval of his beloved's father by rescuing his ship - thus battling the elements, mythical beasts and the sea itself. It was published in 1866, and was dedicated to the channel islands, in which Hugo found such a welcoming home.

Hugo returned to political and social issues in his next novel, *The Man Who Laughs*, which was published in 1869 and painted a critical picture of the aristocracy. The novel was not as successful as his previous efforts, and Hugo himself began to comment on the growing distance between himself and literary contemporaries such as Flaubert and Émile Zola, whose realist and naturalist novels were now exceeding the popularity of his own work. After the Siege of Paris, Hugo lived again in Guernsey from 1872 to 1873, before finally returning to France for the remainder of his life. His last novel, *Ninety-Three*, published in 1874, dealt with a subject that Hugo had previously avoided: the Reign of Terror during the French Revolution. Though Hugo's popularity was on the decline at the time of its publication, many now consider *Ninety-Three* to be a work on par with his earlier and better-known novels.

When Hugo returned to Paris in 1870, the country hailed him as a national hero. This was a sad time for the ageing writer however, as within a brief period he suffered a mild stoke, his daughter Adèle's internment in an insane asylum, and the death of his two sons. His wife Adèle had died in 1868. Hugo's mistress, Juliette Drouet, also died in 1883 – two years before Hugo's own death. Despite this, to honour the fact that he was entering his eightieth year, in 1882, one of the greatest tributes to a living writer was held. The celebrations began on 25th June when Hugo was presented with a Sèvres vase, the traditional gift for sovereigns, and on 27th June one of the largest parades in French history was held.

Victor Hugo's death from pneumonia on 22nd May 1885, at the age of eighty-three, generated intense national mourning. He was not only revered as a towering figure in literature, but he was also a statesman who shaped the Third Republic and democracy in France. More than two million people joined his funeral procession in Paris from the Arc de Triomphe to the Panthéon, where he was buried. He shares a crypt within the with Alexandre Dumas and Émile Zola.

ESMERALDA

DRAMATIS PERSONÆ

- ESMERALDA.
- PHŒBUS DE CHATEAUPERS.
- CLAUDE FROLLO.
- QUASIMODO.
- FLEUR-DE-LYS.
- MADAME ALOISE DE GONDELAURIER.
- DIANA.
- BÉRANGÈRE.
- VISCOUNT DE GIF.
- M. DE CHEVREUSE.
- M. DE MORLAIX.
- CLOPIN FROUILLEFOU.
- THE TOWN-CRIER.

Populace, Vagrants, Archers, etc.

ESMERALDA

ACT I

SCENE.—*The Court of Miracles. It is night. A crowd of vagrants. Noisy dancing. Male and female beggars in different attitudes of their profession. The King of Thune on his cask. Fires, lights, torches. In the shadow a circle of wretched dwellings*

SCENE I

CLAUDE FROLLO, CLOPIN FROUILLEFOU, *then* ESMERALDA, *then* QUASIMODO. THE VAGRANTS

CHORUS OF VAGRANTS.
Long live Clopin! Long live the King of Thune!
Long live the rogues of Paris.
Let us strike our blows at dusk—
The hour when all the cats are drunk.
Let us dance! Defy Pope and bull,
And let us laugh in our skins,

13

Whether April wets or June burns
The feathers in our caps.
Let us smell from afar
The shot of the avenging archer,
Or the bag of money which passes
On the back of the traveler.
In the light of the moon,
We will go dance with the spirits.
Long live Clopin, King of Thune!
Long live the rogues of Paris!

CLAUDE FROLLO (*apart behind a pillar in a corner of the stage. He is covered with a long cloak which hides his priestly garb*).

In the midst of this infamous band
What matters the sigh of a soul?
I suffer! Oh, never did fiercer flame
Burn in the bowels of a volcano.

[ESMERALDA *enters, dancing.*

CHORUS.

There she is! There she is! It is she—Esmeralda!

CLAUDE FROLLO (*aside*).

It is she! oh, yes—'tis she!
Wherefore, relentless fate,
Made you her so beautiful,
Me—so unfortunate?

[*She reaches the center of the stage. The Vagrants form an admiring circle around her.*

ESMERALDA.

An orphan am I,
Child of woe,

To you I turn
And flowers throw!
In my wild joy
Sad sighs abide;
I show a smile,
The tears I hide.

Poor girl—I dance
Where brooklets run,
As chirp the birds
My song flows on:
I am the dove
Which, hurt, must fall;
Over my cradle
Hangs death's pall.

CHORUS.
    Young girl, dance on!
    More gentle you make us.
    Take us for family,
    And play with us,
    As stoops the nightingale
    Unto the sea,
    Teasing its waves
    To ecstasy.

'Tis the young girl—
Child of woe,
When beams her eye
Grief must go.
She's like the bee

Which trembling flies
To the flower's heart,
Its Paradise.

Young girl, dance on!
More gentle you make us.
Take us for family,
And play with us!

CLAUDE FROLLO (*aside*).

Tremble, young girl—
The priest is jealous.

[CLAUDE *attempts to draw near to* ESMERALDA; *she turns away from him with a kind of horror. The procession of the Pope of Fools enters. Torches, lanterns and music. In the middle of the procession, upon a litter surrounded with candles,* QUASIMODO, *decked with cope and miter, is carried.*

CHORUS.

Salute him, clerks of Vasoche!
Shell-heaps, lubbers, beggars!
Salute him, all of you! He comes.
Behold the Pope of Fools!

CLAUDE FROLLO (*perceiving* Quasimodo, *and starting toward him with a gesture of anger*).

Quasimodo! What a strange part to play!
Profanation! Here—Quasimodo!

QUASIMODO.

Great God! what do I hear?

CLAUDE FROLLO.

Come here, I tell you.

QUASIMODO (*jumping from the litter*).

Here I am!

CLAUDE FROLLO.

Be anathematized!

QUASIMODO.

God! it is himself!

CLAUDE FROLLO.

Outrageous audacity!

QUASIMODO.

Moment of terror.

CLAUDE FROLLO.

To your knees, traitor!

QUASIMODO.

Pardon me, Master!

CLAUDE FROLLO.

No! I am a priest.

[CLAUDE FROLLO *tears off* QUASIMODO's *pontifical ornaments, and crushes them underfoot.* THE VAGRANTS *begin to murmur; they form menacing groups around him; he looks at them angrily.*

THE VAGRANTS.

He threatens us,

O comrades!

Here in this place,

Where we reign.

QUASIMODO.

What means the audacity

Of these robbers?

They menace him,

But we shall see!

CLAUDE FROLLO.

Race unclean,

You menace me.

Robbers—Jews—

But we shall see!

[*The anger of* THE VAGRANTS *bursts forth.*

THE VAGRANTS.

Stop! stop! stop!

Down with the mar-joy!

He shall pay for it with his head;

In vain he defends himself.

QUASIMODO.

Have respect for his head.

Let every one cease,

Or I change this festival

To a bloody battle.

CLAUDE FROLLO.

It is not about his head

That Frollo is troubled.

[*Puts his hand on his heart.*

There is the tempest,

There is the battle!

[*At the moment when* THE VAGRANTS' *fury has reached its highest pitch,* CLOPIN FROUILLEFOU *appears at the back of the stage.*

CLOPIN.

Who in this infamous den

Dares to attack my lord the Archdeacon,

And Quasimodo, bell-ringer

Of Notre Dame?

THE VAGRANTS (*subsiding*).

It is Clopin, our King!

CLOPIN.

Clowns! Be off!

THE VAGRANTS.

We must obey!

CLOPIN.

Leave us!

[THE VAGRANTS *retire to their hovels. The Court of Miracles appears deserted.* CLOPIN *approaches* CLAUDE *cautiously.*

SCENE II

CLAUDE FROLLO, QUASIMODO, CLOPIN FROUILLEFOU

CLOPIN.

What purpose brings you to this orgy?

Has your lordship any orders to give me?

You are my master in sorcery;

Speak—I will do all.

CLAUDE FROLLO (*grasping* CLOPIN'S *arm excitedly, and dragging him to the front of the stage*).

I have come to end all.

Listen!

CLOPIN.

My lord!

CLAUDE FROLLO.

I love her more than ever.

You behold me quivering with love and with anguish.

I must have her to-night.

CLOPIN.

You will see her pass by here—in a moment;

It is the way to her home.

CLAUDE FROLLO (*aside*).

Oh! Hell has hold of me!

[*Aloud.*] Soon—you say?

CLOPIN.

Upon the instant!

CLAUDE FROLLO.

Alone?

CLOPIN.

Alone.

CLAUDE FROLLO.

That is enough.

CLOPIN.

Will you wait?

CLAUDE FROLLO.

I wait—Let me have her, or let me die!

CLOPIN.

Can I help you?

CLAUDE FROLLO.

No!

[*He motions to* CLOPIN *to leave him, after having thrown him his purse. When he finds himself alone with* QUASIMODO, *he draws him to the front of the stage.*

CLAUDE FROLLO.

Come! I need you!

QUASIMODO.

It is well!

CLAUDE FROLLO.

For a deed that is impious, frightful, awful!

QUASIMODO.

You are my lord and master!

CLAUDE FROLLO.

Chains, death, the law—We brave them all.

QUASIMODO.

Count upon me.

CLAUDE FROLLO (*recklessly*).

I mean to abduct the gypsy!

QUASIMODO.

Master, take my blood—without telling me why!

[*Upon a sign from* Claude Frollo *he retires up stage and leaves his master down stage.*

CLAUDE FROLLO.

Oh, Heaven! to have given one's mind to the depths,

To have tried all the crimes of sorcery,

To have fallen lower than hell itself:

A priest, at midnight, in the dark to watch for a woman!

And to reflect that in this state in which I find my soul God

sees me!

Well! what does it matter?

Fate drags me on!

Its hand is too strong,

Its will be done!

I begin life over—
The priest insane
Feels hope no longer,
Knows terror is vain!
Demon, who drugs me,
Give her to me;
And I, who evoked thee,
Thy slave will be—
Receive the priest
Whose bonds are riven!
Hell with her
Will be my heaven!
Come, exquisite woman,
Your beauty I claim.
You shall own me forever—
I swear, in God's name!
Since he—since the master
By whom love was given,
Bids me choose—me, a priest,
Between passion and heaven!

QUASIMODO (*returning*).

Master, the moment is at hand!

CLAUDE FROLLO.

Yes—the solemn hour:It will decide my fate. Be silent! Hush!

CLAUDE FROLLO *and* QUASIMODO.

The night is dark,
Footsteps I hear:
In shadow does not
Some one draw near?

[*They go to the back of the stage to listen.*

22

THE WATCH (*passing behind the houses*).

   Vigilance and peace!

   Whoever passes here

   Must ope the eye to darkness,

   To silence strain the ear.

CLAUDE FROLLO *and* QUASIMODO.

   In shadow they come;

   They make no sound:

   Still let us be

   While the watch goes round!

   [*The voices of the watch grow fainter.*

QUASIMODO.

   The watch has passed!

CLAUDE FROLLO.

   Our terror follows it.

   [CLAUDE FROLLO *and* QUASIMODO *look anxiously at the door through which* ESMERALDA *must pass.*

QUASIMODO.

   Love inspires,

   Hope renders strong,

   Him who watches

   While sleeps the throng.

   I see her come—

   Lo! she appears.

   Maid divine!

   Have no fears!

CLAUDE FROLLO.

   Love inspires,

   Hope renders strong,

   Him who watches

While sleeps the throng.

I see her come,

Maid divine!

Lo! she appears—

She is mine!

[ESMERALDA *enters: they throw themselves upon her and try to drag her away: she struggles.*

ESMERALDA.

Help—help! To me—help!

CLAUDE FROLLO *and* QUASIMODO.

Hush, young maiden—hush!

SCENE III

ESMERALDA, QUASIMODO, PHŒBUS DE CHATEAUPERS, *the archers of the watch*

PHŒBUS (*entering at the head of a body of archers*).

In the King's name!

[*In the struggle* CLAUDE *escapes. The archers seize* QUASIMODO.

PHŒBUS.

Arrest him! hold him close!

Be he lord or valet!

At once—we will conduct him

To the prison Chatelet.

[*The archers take* QUASIMODO *up stage and off.* ESMERALDA, *recovered from her fright, approaches* PHŒBUS *with curiosity, mingled with admiration, and draws him gently to the front of the stage.*

ESMERALDA (*to* Phœbus).

Deign to tell me
Your name, sir!
I beg you to.

PHŒBUS.

Phœbus, my child—
Of the family
Of Chateaupers.

ESMERALDA.

Captain?

PHŒBUS.

Yes, my queen!

ESMERALDA.

Queen? oh, no!

PHŒBUS.

Exquisite grace!

ESMERALDA.

Phœbus! I like your name!

PHŒBUS.

Upon my soul
I have a blade
Which has, Madame,
Great havoc made.

ESMERALDA (*to* Phœbus).

A beautiful captain,
An officer grand,
With corselet of steel
And an air of command!
Often, kind sir,

Our hearts they break,
And only laugh
At the tears they make.
PHŒBUS (*aside*).
With a beautiful captain,
An officer gay,
Love hardly succeeds
In living a day.
All soldiers desire
To pluck every rose,
Joys without troubles,
Love without woes.
PHŒBUS (*to* Esmeralda).
A radiant spirit
Smiles at me
Through thine eyes.
ESMERALDA.
A beautiful captain,
An officer grand,
With corselet of steel
And an air of command!
Long watches the girl
He carelessly passed;
And the dreams he awakened
Forever may last!
PHŒBUS.
With a beautiful captain,
An officer gay,
Love hardly succeeds
In a living day!

It's like lightning which flashes—
This eager desire
Which the eyes of sweet maidens
Kindle to fire!

ESMERALDA (*standing before the* Captain *and admiring him*).

My lord Phœbus! Let me see you!
Let me admire you a hundred-fold!
Oh the beautiful scarf of silk—
Oh the fine scarf with fringe of gold!

[PHŒBUS *takes it off and offers it to her.*

PHŒBUS.

Does it please you?

ESMERALDA (*taking the scarf and putting it on*).

Yes, it is beautiful!

PHŒBUS.

One moment!

[*He goes to her and tries to embrace her.*

ESMERALDA (*drawing back*).

Don't, I beg you!

PHŒBUS (*insisting*).

You must kiss me!

ESMERALDA (*drawing away still more*).

No, truly!

PHŒBUS (*laughing*).

A beauty
So cruel,
So haughty,
Is charming.

ESMERALDA.

No, beautiful captain,

In vain you plead!
Can I tell how far
A kiss might lead?

PHŒBUS.

I am a captain,
Why abuse me?
I want a kiss—
Don't refuse me!
Give it me—give it, or I will take!

ESMERALDA.

No, leave me! I beg of you, for my sake.

PHŒBUS.

One kiss, one kiss—'tis nothing, you see.

ESMERALDA.

Nothing to you, but much to me!

PHŒBUS.

Look at me, dear! I am playing no part!

ESMERALDA.

Alas, but I cannot look into my heart!

PHŒBUS.

To-night love shall make an entrance there!

ESMERALDA.

Wherever love enters, soon follows despair.

[*She slips out of his arms and escapes.* PHŒBUS, *disappointed, turns to* QUASIMODO, *whom the archers hold bound at the back of the stage.*

PHŒBUS.

She escapes me, she resists me!
A gay adventure, verily!
I keep the worst of our two birds of prey—

The owl remains; the nightingale flew away!
[*He places himself at the head of his guard and goes out, taking* QUASIMODO *with him.*
CHORUS OF THE WATCH.
    Vigilance and peace—
    Whoever passes here
    Must ope the eye to darkness,
    To silence strain the ear!
    [*The sound grows fainter and finally ceases.*

ACT II

SCENE.—The square of Grève. The pillory. Quasimodo *is in the pillory. Populace on the square*

SCENE I

CHORUS.

    He abducted a girl—

    What! is it possible?

    Hark! how they abuse him!

    Do you hear, my friends?

    Quasimodo has been hunting on Cupid's domain!

A WOMAN OF THE PEOPLE.

    He will pass through my street

    On his return from the pillory;

    And it is Pierrat Forterne

    Who will give us the signal.

TOWN-CRIER.

    In the King's name, whom God protect!

    The man you see here, will be put

    Under a strong guard,

    In the pillory for one hour.

CHORUS.

    Down with him! Down with him!

    The hunchback, the deaf, the one-eyed creature

This Barabbas!

I believe, s'death! he's looking at us.

Down with the sorcerer!

He makes faces, he kicks;

He makes dogs bark in the streets.

Punish the rascal well!

Double the whip and the penalty.

QUASIMODO.

Drink!

CHORUS.

Hang him!

QUASIMODO.

Drink!

CHORUS.

Be accursed!

[ESMERALDA, *some instants ago, joined the crowd. She perceives* QUASIMODO, *first with surprise, then with pity. Suddenly, in the midst of all the noise, she mounts the pillory, unfastens a little cup which she carries on her belt, and gives a drink to* QUASIMODO.

CHORUS.

What are you doing, beautiful girl?

Leave Quasimodo alone!

When Beelzebub roasts,

Nobody gives him water.

[*She comes down. The archers unfasten* Quasimodo *and take him away.*

CHORUS.

He abducted a woman!

Who? This dolt!

It is terrible, it is infamous,

It is too much!

Do you hear, my friends?

Quasimodo

Dared to go hunting on Cupid's domain.

SCENE II

*A magnificent drawing-room in which people are making
preparations for a festival.* PHŒBUS, FLEUR-DE-LYS, MADAME
ALOISE DE GONDELAURIER

MADAME ALOISE.

Phœbus, my future son-in-law, listen to me. I am fond of you.

Be master here, as if you were another self.

Look to it that every one is gay to-night.

And you, my daughter, come, get ready.

You will be the most beautiful at this festival,

Be also the most happy.

[*She goes up stage and gives orders to the servants, who
continue the preparations.*

FLEUR-DE-LYS.

Sir, since the other week,

We have hardly seen you twice!

This festival brings you back.

How fortunate for us!

PHŒBUS.

Don't scold, I beg of you!

FLEUR-DE-LYS.

I understand. Phœbus forgets me!

PHŒBUS.

I swear to you—

FLEUR-DE-LYS.

Don't swear! They only swear who deceive.

PHŒBUS.

Forget you? What folly!

Are you not the most fair?

Am I not the most loving?

PHŒBUS (*aside*).

My beautiful betrothed

Is out of sorts to-day;

Suspicion is in her mind.

What a pity!

Beauties, the lovers you treat ill

Go elsewhere.

You can do more with pleasure

Than with tears.

FLEUR-DE-LYS (*aside*).

To betray me, his betrothed,

Who belong to him!

I, who have only him to think of

And worry about!

Ah! whether he is away or here,

What grief!

Present, he scorns my joy;

Absent, my tears.

FLEUR-DE-LYS.

Phœbus, the scarf that I worked for you—

What have you done with it? I don't see it.

PHŒBUS (*troubled*).

The scarf? I don't know!

[*Aside.*] Good God! unlucky chance!

FLEUR-DE-LYS.

You forgot it?

[*Aside.*]To whom has he given it?

And for whom am I deserted?

MADAME ALOISE (*coming up to them and trying to reconcile them*).

Heavens! get married! Then you can quarrel.

PHŒBUS (*to* FLEUR-DE-LYS).

No! I have not forgotten it.

I remember, I carefully folded it

And put it in an enameled box

That I had made for it.

[*Passionately to* FLEUR-DE-LYS, *who still frets.*

I swear I love you better

Than one could love Venus herself!

FLEUR-DE-LYS.

Don't swear! Don't swear!

They only swear who deceive!

MADAME ALOISE.

Children, don't quarrel—everything is bright to-day!

Come, my daughter, you must be seen!

The guests are coming! Everything has its turn.

[*To the servants.*] Light the candles and let the ball begin.

I want everything to be beautiful, to seem as bright as day.

PHŒBUS.

Since we have Fleur-de-lys, nothing is wanting to the ball.

FLEUR-DE-LYS.

   Yes, Phœbus—love is wanting! [*They go out.*

PHŒBUS (*watching* Fleur-de-lys *go out*).

   She speaks the truth: my heart is sad
   Even when she is near—
   The one I love, the one who fills my soul—
   Alas! she is not here.

   Exquisite creature,
   To you my love!
   Oh, dancing shadow,
   My sweet-voiced dove,
   Absent, yet with me
   Wherever I move!

   She's as bewildering and sweet
   As is a nest 'mid rushes,
   Sweet as a rosebud crowned with moss,
   Sweet as the joy which sorrow hushes.

   Humble child and virgin proud,
   Soul that's pure though free!
   Voluptuous ardors sink abashed
   Before thy chastity.

   In the dark night she comes,
   An angel from the skies;
   Her forehead veiled by shadows,
   Flames darting from her eyes.

I see her face forever—
Now bright, now dark it seems;
But strangely—'tis in heaven
I see her in these dreams.

Exquisite creature.
To you my love!
Oh, dancing shadow,
My sweet-voiced dove,
Absent, yet with me
Wherever I move!

[*Enter several lords and ladies in gala dress.*

SCENE III

The preceding. Viscount de Gif, M. de Morlaix, M. de
Chevreuse, Madame de Gondelaurier, Fleur-de-lys,
Diana, Bérangère. *Ladies, Lords*

VISCOUNT DE GIF.
  My salutations, noble hostesses!
MADAME ALOISE, PHŒBUS, FLEUR-DE-LYS (*bowing*).
  Good-evening, noble viscount!
  Forget all care and grief
  Beneath this hospitable roof.
M. DE MORLAIX.
  Ladies, may God send you

Health, pleasure, and happiness!

MADAME ALOISE, PHŒBUS, FLEUR-DE-LYS.

May Heaven return with interest

All your good wishes, my lord!

M. DE CHEVREUSE.

Ladies, from the bottom of my soul

I belong to you, as I do to God!

MADAME ALOISE, PHŒBUS, FLEUR-DE-LYS.

Kind sir, may our good Lady

Come always to your aid!

[*All the guests enter.*

CHORUS.

Come to the festival, come!

Page, lordship, and ladyship, come!

With flowers in your hand,

A joy-seeking band,

Come to the festival, come!

[*The guests greet and salute each other; servants circulate among the crowd, bearing platters laden with flowers and fruits. A group of young girls forms itself near a window to the left. Suddenly one of them calls to the others, and motions to them to look out of the window.*

DIANA (*looking out*).

Come and look! come and look, Bérangère!

BÉRANGÈRE (*looking into the street*).

Isn't she quick? Isn't she light?

DIANA.

It is a fairy or it is love.

VISCOUNT DE GIF (*laughing*).

Who dances in the public square?

M. DE CHEVREUSE (*after having looked*).

    Indeed! it is the magician.

    Phœbus, it is your gypsy

    Whom, the other night, with valor

    You saved from a robber.

VISCOUNT DE GIF.

    Oh, yes, it is the gypsy.

M. DE MORLAIX.

    She's as beautiful as the day.

DIANA (*to* Phœbus).

    If you know her, tell her to come

    And dance for us.

PHŒBUS (*looking out with an absent air*).

    It might be she!

    [*To* M. DE GIF.] Do you think she would remember?

FLEUR-DE-LYS (*who watches and listens*).

    Every one remembers you.

    Come, call her, tell her to come up.

    [*Aside.*] I will see whether to believe what I am told.

PHŒBUS (*to* Fleur-de-lys).

    You wish it? Well, let us try!

    [*He motions to the dancer to come up.*

THE YOUNG GIRLS.

    She is coming!

M. DE CHEVREUSE.

    She has disappeared under the porch.

DIANA.

    She has left the mob, stupefied.

VISCOUNT DE GIF.

    Ladies, you will see the nymph of the streets.

FLEUR-DE-LYS (*aside*).

How quickly she obeyed that sign from Phœbus!

SCENE IV

The same. ESMERALDA. *The gypsy enters timidly, confused and radiant. Movement of admiration. The crowd falls back before her*

CHORUS.

Look! her brow is fair amid the fairest,

As a star would shine, surrounded by torches.

PHŒBUS.

Oh, creature divine!

Admiration is duty.

Of this ball she is queen,

Her crown is her beauty.

[*He turns to* MESSIEURS DE GIF *and* DE CHEVREUSE.

Friends, my soul is on fire.

War and death would I face,

To hold in my arms

Such bewildering grace.

M. DE CHEVREUSE.

She is a heavenly vision,

A dream most rare and tender,

Which, floating through earth's darkness,

Radiates celestial splendor.

Born in the public streets—
Oh, blind caprice of fate,
To trail through muddy streams
A flower so immaculate!

ESMERALDA (*fixing her eyes on* PHŒBUS *in the crowd*).

It is my Phœbus, I was sure,
Just as that night I found him;
Whether in satin or in steel,
How grace and strength surround him!
Phœbus—my head is all on fire,
All burns within me, joy and pain;
My soul's consumed for lack of tears,
Just as earth yearns for rain.

FLEUR-DE-LYS.

How fair she is—yes, I was sure!
Jealous, indeed, I ought to be;
But yet to match that loveliness
How great must be my jealousy!
Alas! perhaps we both, foredoomed
To waste 'neath sorrow's harsh caress,
Full soon shall die—she in her flower,
I in my loneliness!

MADAME ALOISE.

A radiant creature, truly,
But, faith, 'tis a disgrace
That such a wretched gypsy
Should have so sweet a face.
Alas! the curious laws of fate
'Tis not for mortal mind to know:
The serpent hides his treacherous head

Beneath the fairest flowers that grow.

ALL (*together*).

    She has the calmness, the delight

    Of radiant skies on a warm night.

MADAME ALOISE (*to* Esmeralda).

    Come, child! My beauty, come—

    Come and dance us some new dance!

    [ESMERALDA *prepares to dance, and draws from her bosom the scarf which* PHŒBUS *gave her.*

FLEUR DE-LYS.

    My scarf! Phœbus, you have deceived me!

    My rival! Here she is!

    [FLEUR-DE-LYS *snatches the scarf from* ESMERALDA, *and falls in a swoon. All the people rush angrily toward the gypsy, who flies for protection to* PHŒBUS.

ALL.

    Is it true that Phœbus loves her?

    Infamous creature, go—depart!

    To brave us thus in our own home,

    You must have an audacious heart.

    Oh! height of insolence! Retire!

    Go back into the public street!

    The common tradesmen, they can praise

    The jumping of your low-born feet.

    Away with her, away at once!

    Out at the door! 'Tis a disgrace

    For this degraded girl to lift

    Her eyes to such a lofty place.

ESMERALDA.

    Oh, defend me! Help! Defend me,

Save me, Phœbus, I implore thee;
For the poor forsaken gypsy,
Stands defenseless now before thee!
PHŒBUS.
I love her, and I love but her.
Yes! her defender I will be.
I'll fight for her, and my strong arm
Will bear my heart out valiantly.
If some one must be her protector,
I am the one—and doubt me not,
Her wrongs are mine, and who insults her
Must answer for it on the spot.
ALL.
What! She is what he loves! Indeed!
Away from here, away from here!
A gypsy he prefers to us;
With loving words he calms her fear.
Hush! silence! Both of you be still!
No further words of insolence.
[*To* PHŒBUS.] From you, 'tis too much arrogance!
[*To* ESMERALDA.] From thee, too much impertinence!
[PHŒBUS *and his friends protect the gypsy, who is menaced by all the guests of* MADAME DE GONDELAURIER. ESMERALDA *staggers toward the door.*

ACT III

SCENE.—*The front yard of a tavern. Tavern to the right; trees to the left. In the back a door, and a small low wall which closes in the yard. In the distance the roof of Notre Dame with its towers and its spire. A dark silhouette of old Paris outlines itself against the red sunset. The river Seine is at the base of the picture*

SCENE I

PHŒBUS, VISCOUNT DE GIF, M. DE MORLAIX, M. DE CHEVREUSE, *and many other friends of* PHŒBUS, *seated at tables, are drinking, and singing; afterward* DON CLAUDE FROLLO

CHORUS.
>Be propitious and well-inclined,
>Our Lady of Saint Lo,
>To him who only water hates
>Of all things here below!

PHŒBUS.
>Give to the brave
>In every place
>A well-filled cellar,
>A pretty face.

43

Happy fellow!
Help him hold
Dainty women,
Wine that's old.

If a beauty
Of cold mien
Be unwilling,
'Tis sometimes seen,
He jokes with her
With merry winks,
Then he sings,
Then he drinks!

The day goes by.
Or drunk or not,
He soon embraces
His Toinotte;
Then ferocious
He goes to bed
In a cannon's mouth,
And sleeps like lead!

And his soul,
Which often seems
To mix up women
With his dreams,
Is contented if the wind,
With its come and go,
Rocks the canvas of his tent

Gently to and fro!

CHORUS.

Be propitious and well inclined,

Our Lady of Saint Lo!

To him who only water hates

Of all things here below.

[*Enter* CLAUDE FROLLO, *who seats himself at a table at some distance from* PHŒBUS, *and appears at first to observe nothing that passes around him.*

VISCOUNT DE GIF (*to* Phœbus).

That pretty gypsy,

What are you doing with her?

[CLAUDE FROLLO *makes a movement of attention.*

PHŒBUS.

To-night, in an hour,

I have a meeting with her.

ALL.

Truly?

PHŒBUS.

Truly!

[*The agitation of* CLAUDE FROLLO *increases.*

VISCOUNT DE GIF.

In one hour?

PHŒBUS.

In one moment!

Oh, love! supremest rapture!

To feel one heart holds two!

To own the woman that one loves—

Be slave and conqueror too!

To have her soul; to have her charms,

Her song which fills with bliss;
To see her sweet eyes wet with tears,
To dry them with a kiss.
[*While he sings, the others drink and strike their glasses.*
CHORUS.
'Tis a rapture supreme,
Whatever one thinks,
To drink to one's love,
And to love what one drinks!
PHŒBUS.
Friends, the prettiest of all,
A grace divine,
Oh, wonder, ecstasy!
Friends, she is mine!
CLAUDE FROLLO (*aside*).
I bind myself to hell;
Misfortune on you dwell!
PHŒBUS.
Pleasure awaits us;
Exhaust without remorse
The better part of life,
Love's precious intercourse!
What matter if one dies,
When joy has passed away,
I'd give a century for an hour,
Eternity for a day.
[*The curfew rings; the friends of* PHŒBUS *arise from the table, replace their swords, their caps, their cloaks, and prepare to depart.*

CHORUS.

  Phœbus, the hour is come;
  It is the curfew-bell:
  Hurry to your beloved;
  God's blessing on you dwell!

PHŒBUS.

  At last the hour is come;
  It is the curfew-bell.
  I go to my beloved;
  God's blessing on her dwell!
  [*The friends of* PHŒBUS *go out.*

SCENE II

CLAUDE FROLLO, PHŒBUS. CLAUDE FROLLO *stops* PHŒBUS
as he is about to go out

CLAUDE FROLLO.

  Captain!

PHŒBUS.

  Who is this man?

CLAUDE FROLLO.

  Listen to me?

PHŒBUS.

  Make haste!

CLAUDE FROLLO.

  Do you know the name of the oneWho awaits you at the
  meeting to-night?

PHŒBUS.

By my life, it is my beauty!

The one I love and who loves me.

My song-bird, my dancing gypsy,

My Esmeralda, it is she!

CLAUDE FROLLO.

It is death!

PHŒBUS.

Friend! First, you are an idiot;

Second, go to the devil!

CLAUDE FROLLO.

Listen!

PHŒBUS.

What do I care?

CLAUDE FROLLO.

Phœbus, if you cross the threshold of that door—

PHŒBUS.

You are mad!

CLAUDE FROLLO.

You are dead!

Tremble! One of the gypsies she!

No law protects those awful places.

There love's a masquerade for hate,

Death lies concealed in their embraces.

PHŒBUS (*laughing*).

My dear sir, readjust your cape,

Return unto your fools' retreat!

Strange they allow you to escape!

May Esculapius, Jupiter, the Devil,

Thither conduct your straying feet!

CLAUDE FROLLO.

Truly they are faithless women;

Believe that the report speaks true.

Darkness strange and deep surrounds them;

Phœbus! there death waits for you!

[CLAUDE FROLLO'S *earnestness seems to trouble* PHŒBUS, *who looks at his interrogator with anxiety.*

PHŒBUS.

He astounds me!

Ah, he wounds me,

In spite of myself, with doubt!

This city great

Is full of hate,

And treachery is all about!

CLAUDE FROLLO.

I astound him,

And I wound him,

In spite of himself, with doubt.

The fool, he fears,

And sees and hears

Nothing but treachery about.

Believe me—my lord, avoid the siren

Who lures you to destruction.

More than one gypsy in her rage

Has stabbed a heart palpitating with love.

[PHŒBUS, *whom he tries to drag along, recovers himself and pushes him off.*

PHŒBUS.

Have I become a fool?

Gypsy, Jewess, or Moor,

The love that questions what she be
Is love most base and poor.
The fateful hour is come,
Unto my love I fly!
If death be but as sweet as she,
It will be fine to die!

CLAUDE FROLLO (*holding him*).

Consider! A gypsy!
Your folly is great.
How dare you thus rashly
Trifle with fate!
Oh, dread the false creature
Who waits in the gloom,
And do not thus wildly
Rush to your doom.

[PHŒBUS *exits quickly, in spite of* CLAUDE FROLLO. CLAUDE FROLLO *stands gloomy and undecided for a moment; then follows* PHŒBUS.

SCENE III

A chamber. In the background, a window which opens on the river. CLOPIN FROUILLEFOU *enters, bearing a torch. He is followed by several men, to whom he makes a preconcerted sign, and places them in a dark corner, in which they disappear; then he returns to the door and signals to some one to come up.*
DON CLAUDE *appears*

CLOPIN (*to* Claude).

From here you can see the captain

And the gypsy without being seen.

[*He shows him an alcove behind some tapestry.*

CLAUDE FROLLO.

The men are stationed and ready?

CLOPIN.

They are ready.

CLAUDE FROLLO.

The projector of this must never be known.

Silence! take this purse.

I will give you as much more afterward.

[CLAUDE FROLLO *hides himself in the alcove.* CLOPIN *exits with caution.* ESMERALDA *and* PHŒBUS *enter.*

CLAUDE FROLLO (*aside*).

Oh, woman adored,

Destiny's prey!

She enters in beauty,

In tears goes away.

ESMERALDA (*to* Phœbus).

My lord the count,

My feelings I try to hide.

My heart is filled with shame,

And filled also with pride.

PHŒBUS (*to* Esmeralda).

My beauty, white and red,

I beg you blush no more.

Love, entering love's domain,

Leaves fear outside the door.

[PHŒBUS *makes* ESMERALDA *sit down on the bench beside*

him.

PHŒBUS.

    Dost thou love me?

ESMERALDA.

    I love thee!

CLAUDE FROLLO (*aside*).

    What torture!

PHŒBUS.

    The adorable creature!

    Upon my soul, you are divine!

ESMERALDA.

    Your lips are flatterers;

    You make me feel ashamed.

    I beg of you, don't come so near.

CLAUDE FROLLO.

    They love each other. How I envy them!

ESMERALDA.

    My Phœbus! I owe my life to you.

PHŒBUS.

    And I—I owe my happiness to you.

ESMERALDA.

    Be good to me!

    Oh, try to be

    Gentle, I entreat,

    To the young maid,

    Who much afraid

    Trembles at your feet!

PHŒBUS.

    Oh, my white queen,

    Goddess serene,

Sovereign of beauty,
Whose bright eyes shine
With fires divine
Of passion and of duty!

CLAUDE FROLLO.

I wait for them;
I hark to them.
How tender she,
How handsome he!
How near their doom!
Be joyous he,
And happy she,
While I prepare their tomb!

PHŒBUS.

Nymph or woman,
Saint or human,
Be my wife to me!
All day I yearn,
All night I burn,
Such is my love for thee!

ESMERALDA.

I am woman,
I am human,
And my soul afire,
Trembles ever,
Longs forever,
As throbs a lover's lyre!

CLAUDE FROLLO.

Woman, wait!
My flame as great,

My blade must have its turn.
Oh! I admire
These souls afire,
And these hearts which burn!
PHŒBUS.
Be always white and red, my love,
And smile at our bright lot;
Smile sweet at love, which we've awaked,
And chastity, which we've forgot.
Your mouth is heaven—my heaven, love—
My soul would cling in bliss
Upon it, love, and pray that life
Might end with one long kiss.
ESMERALDA.
Your voice delights my ear, love;
Your smile is sweet and free.
The laughing passion in your eyes
Benumbs and conquers me.
Your wishes are my law, love,
But I can't yield to this:
My virtue and my happiness
Might die in that long kiss!
CLAUDE FROLLO.
Don't let them hear your step, Death,
As near to them you creep!
My jealous hatred will keep watch
While their love falls asleep.
From out their arms so closely locked
You'll steal away their bliss!
Phœbus—your wish is granted,

You die for that long kiss!

[CLAUDE FROLLO *rushes upon* PHŒBUS *and stabs him; then he opens the window in the back, through which he escapes. With a great cry,* ESMERALDA *falls upon the body of* PHŒBUS. *The men stationed at the corner rush forward, seize her, and seem to accuse her.*

ACT IV

SCENE I

ESMERALDA (*alone, chained, lying upon a bed of straw*).
  What! He in the tomb and I in this cell—
  He a victim and I a prisoner!
  I saw him fall! In truth, he's dead!
  And this crime, this awful crime—
  They say it is my work!
  The stem of our life, while yet green, is broken.
  Phœbus has gone, and he shows me the way.
  Yesterday they made his grave,
  To-morrow they'll make mine!
ROMANCE
  Phœbus, is there nothing left,
  No help given, to those bereft
  In this cruel wise—
  Neither filters, love, nor charms,
  To assuage the soul's alarms,
  Or reopen closèd eyes?

  God in heaven, I adore thee!
  Every hour I implore thee!

Deign to end my life to-day
Or to take my love away!

Phœbus, let us turn our wings
Toward the lights supernal,
Where all things must go at last,
Where love bides and is eternal.
On earth our bodies sleep together,
In heaven our souls will live forever!

God in heaven, I adore thee!
Every hour I implore thee!
Deign to end my life to-day
Or to take my love away!

[*The door opens.* CLAUDE FROLLO *enters, a lamp in his hand, his hood pulled over his face: he comes and stands, motionless, in front of* ESMERALDA.

ESMERALDA (*jumping up with terror*).

Who is this man?

CLAUDE FROLLO (*covered by his hood*).

A priest!

ESMERALDA.

A priest! How mysterious!

CLAUDE FROLLO.

Are you ready?

ESMERALDA.

Ready for what?

CLAUDE FROLLO.

Ready to die.

ESMERALDA.
  Yes.
CLAUDE FROLLO.
  It is well.
ESMERALDA.
  Will it be soon? Answer me, father!
CLAUDE FROLLO.
  Do you suffer so much?
ESMERALDA.
  Yes, I suffer.
CLAUDE FROLLO.
  Perhaps I, who shall live to-morrow,
  Suffer more than you.
ESMERALDA.
  You? Who, then, are you?
CLAUDE FROLLO.
  The tomb lies between us!
ESMERALDA.
  Your name?
CLAUDE FROLLO.
  You wish to know it?
ESMERALDA.
  Yes. [*He lifts his hood.*
  The priest!
  It is the priest! O God! my feeble strength inspire!
  It is indeed his brow of ice, it is his glance of fire!
  'Tis he who has pursued me, remorseless, day and night;
  'Twas he who killed my Phœbus, and slew my heart's delight.
  Monster, from my prison, with death's cold hand on me,
  I'll curse thee, till within the grave my lips shall silent be!

What have I done to thee? What is thine awful plan?
What dost thou want with me, relentless, impious man?
You hate me!

CLAUDE FROLLO.

I love you!
I love you—it is infamous!
Oh, shame to my priesthood!
This love, it is my soul;
This love, it is my blood!
At your feet I fall;
Hear my heart, which cries,
I prefer your tomb
Unto Paradise.
Pity me. I love you! Your pity I implore!
For you I've sinned. Have mercy, do not curse me more!

ESMERALDA.

He loves me! Oh, crown of horrors!
He holds me—this horrible sorcerer!

CLAUDE FROLLO.

The only living thing in me
Is my love and my anguish!
Hopeless anguish,
Wretched plight!
Alas! I love her,
Painful night!

ESMERALDA.

Awful moment,
Cruel fright!
Heaven! He loves me,
Fearful night.

CLAUDE FROLLO (*aside*).

    She shudders, quivers in my arms;

    The priest has won his chance at last!

    By night I bore her, once, away;

    Now, in the day, I'll hold her fast!

    Death, which follows in my train,

    Will give her back to love again!

ESMERALDA.

    Pity—pity, let me go!

    Phœbus is dead; he waits above.

    Alas! I tremble, I'm afraid,

    I shiver at your frightful love,

    E'en as the bird which, tortured, dies

    Beneath the vulture's cruel eyes!

CLAUDE FROLLO.

    Accept me, I love you! Refuse me no more!

    Have pity for me, for yourself, I implore!

ESMERALDA.

    Your prayer is an insult.

CLAUDE FROLLO.

    Would you rather die?

ESMERALDA.

    The body dies—the soul lives!

CLAUDE FROLLO.

    To die is terrible!

ESMERALDA.

    Hush! your impious words!

    Your love makes death beautiful!

CLAUDE FROLLO.

    Choose! choose! Or Claude or death!

[Claude *falls at* ESMERALDA's *feet in supplication. She repels him.*

ESMERALDA.

No, murderer, I will not! Hush!
A crime is this foul love you've nursed.
Better the tomb to which I fly—
Be cursed amid the most accursed!

CLAUDE FROLLO.

Tremble, for the scaffold claims you!
You know not what awful schemes
This breast of fury has engendered;
And hell abets me in my dreams.
How I love thee!
Thy hand give,
And to-morrow
Thou shalt live!
Night benumbed
With terror's breath!
Tears for me,
For thee death!
Say, "I love thee!"
Cease thy scorning;
Thy last day
Is dawning!
Ah! since in vain I supplicate,
In vain thy hate I fight,
Farewell forever! One day more,
Then comes eternal night.

ESMERALDA.

Inhuman priest.

Go! I abhor thee!
His dear blood yet
Seems dripping o'er thee,
Oh, night of horror,
Night of shame!
Enough of tears;
Death I claim!
In prison I brave thee,
In chains defy!
Be thou accursed
Eternally!
Thy passion be thy punishment!
To God my love leads me:
The gates of heaven he'll open,
But hell shall close o'er thee!
[*A jailer appears.* CLAUDE FROLLO *signs to him to lead out* Esmeralda. *He exits while they drag forth the gypsy.*

SCENE II

The area before Notre Dame; the front of the church. The sound of bells is heard

QUASIMODO.
My God! I love,
Except myself,
All that's here—
The air which passes,

And which chases
Away care;
And the swallow
Who is faithful
To the old roof;
The chapels high
O'ershadowed by
The Holy Cross;
Every rose
That grows;
Every sight
Of delight!

Sad creature, I—
Uncouth, ill-made!
None envies me!
This is life
As it is!
Darkest night,
Bluest sky,
What matters it?
Every door
Leads to God.
Ignoble scabbard,
Noble blade;
Fair my soul
God has made.

Ring, bells small and great—
Ring on, ring on!

Mix well your voices,
Gruff and sweet!
In the turrets,
In the tower,
Sing your song!

How they ring!
With all their might,
Let them hum
Day and night!
Our festival shall be
Magnificent, I swear!
Assail it fiercer yet,
The palpitating air!
The stupid peasants run,
And o'er the bridges tear!

Let them ring,
Let them hum,
Day and night!
Every feast
Is increased
By their might!

[*He turns toward the front of the church.*
I saw black hangings in the chapel.
Are they dragging some misery here?
God! a presentiment! I'll not believe it!
[*Enter* CLAUDE FROLLO *and* CLOPIN *without perceiving*
QUASIMODO.

It is my master! I'll observe him. He is gloomy too!
[*He hides himself in an obscure angle of the porch.*
Oh, my mistress! Oh, Notre Dame!
Take my life! save my soul!

SCENE III

QUASIMODO *hidden,* CLAUDE FROLLO, CLOPIN

CLAUDE FROLLO.
So Phœbus is at Montfort?
CLOPIN.
My lord, he is not dead!
CLAUDE FROLLO.
Provided nothing brings him here!
CLOPIN.
Do not fear it;
He is too feeble yet for such a journey.
If he came, 'twould be his death.
My lord, you can feel sure
That every step would reopen his wound;
Do not fear anything this morning.
CLAUDE FROLLO.
Oh! let me hold her just to-day
For life or death within my power!
Hell! I'll give you all the rest,
If you grant me this one hour!
[*To* CLOPIN.] They will soon bring the gypsy here!

You remember everything!
In the square—with your men—
CLOPIN.
    Yes.
CLAUDE FROLLO.
    Keep in the shadow;
    If I cry, "To me!" you come.
CLOPIN.
    Yes!
CLAUDE FROLLO.
    Have plenty with you!
CLOPIN.
    If you cry, "To me!"
CLAUDE FROLLO.
    Yes.
CLOPIN.
    I rush to her,
    I tear her from the King's men—
CLAUDE FROLLO.
    Yes.
CLOPIN.
    And give her to you.
CLAUDE FROLLO.
    Go, mix among the crowd,
    And perhaps she
    Will look upon the priest
    More tenderly;
    Then rush—rush all of you—
CLOPIN.
    Yes, my master!

CLAUDE FROLLO.

Hold yourselves close!

CLOPIN.

Yes.

CLAUDE FROLLO.

Hide your arms,

Not to excite suspicion!

CLOPIN.

Master, you shall see!

CLAUDE FROLLO.

But hell may take her quick,

With my good-will,

If now this insane creature

Refuses still!

Destiny! Oh, fatal stroke!

Friend, I count on thee!

On this my only chance I wait

With fierce anxiety.

CLOPIN.

Fear nothing terrible, my lord,

Count faithfully on me,

And on this last and only chance

Rely courageously!

[*They go out hurriedly. The populace begin to enter the square.*

SCENE IV

The populace; Quasimodo; *afterward* Esmeralda, *and her escort; then* Claude Frollo, Phœbus, Clopin Frouillefou, *priests, archers, officers of the law*

CHORUS.
　　To Notre Dame
　　Come, get a sight
　　Of the young woman
　　Who dies to-night!

　　This gypsy woman
　　Who stabbed, they say,
　　The handsomest officer
　　In the King's pay.

　　In vain did Heaven
　　Beauty lend her!
　　Is it possible—
　　God defend her!—
　　A soul so black,
　　An eye so tender!

　　A frightful thing,
　　Human nature is so!
　　The poor unfortunate!
　　Come, let us go
　　To Notre Dame

To get a sight
Of the young woman
Who dies to-night!

[*The crowd increases; noise; a gloomy procession begins to appear on the Place du Parvis. Rows of black penitents. Banners of La Miséricorde. Torches, archers, officers of the law and the watch. The soldiers disperse the crowd.* ESMERALDA *appears. She wears a chemise; a rope is around her neck; her feet are bare, and she is covered with a long black veil of crape. Following her, come the executioners and the King's officers. As the prisoner reaches the front of the church, a somber chant is heard in the distance, coming from the interior of the church, whose doors are closed.*

CHORUS (*in the church*).

Omnes fluctus fluminis
Transierunt super me
In imo voraginis
Ubi plorant animæ.

[*The chant draws nearer. It bursts forth, at length, when near the doors, which open suddenly and discover the interior of the church. It is filled with a long procession of priests in their robes of ceremony; banners are borne before them.* CLAUDE FROLLO, *in sacerdotal costume, leads the procession. He goes toward the criminal.*

THE PEOPLE.

Alive to-day, to-morrow dead!
Heaven! thy wings around her spread!

ESMERALDA.

It is Phœbus who calls me

Unto our home eternal,
Where God will hold us in His arms,
Safe from misfortunes cruel.
Though plunged in the abyss of woe,
A joyful hope is given:
I am to die upon the earth
To be re-born in heaven!

CLAUDE FROLLO.

To die so young, so beautiful!
Alas! the guilty priest
Must suffer greater woe than she;
He ne'er will be released.
Oh, hapless child of sorrow,
Lost through my infamy,
You only die from off this earth,
While heaven is lost to me!

THE PEOPLE.

Alas! she is an infidel.
God's words, unto us spoken,
Say that in heaven for such as she
No blessed gate shall open.
Death holds her fast, what misery!
She can escape it, never!
She dies unto the world this day,
And unto heaven forever!

[*The procession approaches.* CLAUDE *accosts* ESMERALDA.

ESMERALDA (*frozen with terror*).

It is the priest!

CLAUDE FROLLO (*low*).

Yes, it is I! I love you, I entreat you!

Say but one word! 'Tis not too late;
I can yet save you!
Say, I love you!

ESMERALDA.

I abhor you! Go!

CLAUDE FROLLO.

Then die! I'll go where I can find you!
[Claude *turns to the crowd.*
We deliver this woman to the secular arm;
At this solemn moment may the breath of the Lord
Pass over her soul!
[*As the officers of the law are about to seize* ESMERALDA,
QUASIMODO *jumps into the square, thrusts back the archers,*
takes ESMERALDA *in his arms, and throws himself with her*
into the church.

QUASIMODO.

Sanctuary! sanctuary! sanctuary!

THE PEOPLE.

Sanctuary! sanctuary! sanctuary!
Rejoice, O people!
Hail to the good bell-ringer!

Oh, destiny!
The criminal
Belongs to heaven!
The scaffold falls!
The eternal God
Instead of a tomb
Discloses the altar!
Executioners, back!

King's officers, back!
This barrier
Limits your power.
Thou hast changed
Everything here.
The angels claim her;
She belongs to God!

CLAUDE FROLLO (*commanding silence by a gesture*).
She is not saved! She is a gypsy!
Notre Dame can save none but Christians!
Pagans are proscribed even when clasping the altar!
[*To the King's men.*] In the name of my lord the Archbishop
of Paris,
I give you back this sinful woman!

QUASIMODO (*to the archers*).
I will defend her! I swear it.
Approach us not!

CLAUDE FROLLO (*to the archers*).
Do you hesitate?
Obey me, on the instant!
Tear the gypsy from this holy place.
[*The archers advance.* QUASIMODO *places himself between
them and* ESMERALDA.

QUASIMODO.
Never!
[*A horseman is heard approaching. He calls out:*
Wait! [*The crowd disperses.*

PHŒBUS (*appearing on horseback. He is pale, breathless,
exhausted as is a man who has made a long journey*).
Wait!

ESMERALDA.

Phœbus!

CLAUDE FROLLO (*aside, terrified*).

My plot has failed.

PHŒBUS (*leaping from his horse*).

God be praised! I breathe

And I arrive in time!

This girl is innocent.

Behold my assassin!

[*Points to* CLAUDE FROLLO.

ALL.

Heavens! the priest!

PHŒBUS.

The priest alone is guilty, and I will prove it!

Arrest him!

THE PEOPLE.

Oh, wonder!

[*The archers surround* CLAUDE FROLLO.

CLAUDE FROLLO.

God alone is Master!

ESMERALDA.

Phœbus!

PHŒBUS.

Esmeralda!

[*They fall into each other's arms.*

ESMERALDA.

My adored Phœbus, we shall live!

PHŒBUS.

Thou shalt live!

ESMERALDA.

For us shines happiness!

THE PEOPLE.

Live, both of you!

ESMERALDA.

Hear these joyous shouts!

At thy feet receive me, humble girl!

Heavens! thou art pale! What is the matter?

PHŒBUS (*staggering*).

I die!

[*She catches him in her arms. Expectation and anxiety among the crowd.*

Each step I took toward you, my beloved,

Reopened my wound, that was hardly healed.

I have taken your grave and given you life.

I die! Destiny has avenged thee.

My angel, I go to see

If heaven is worth thy love!

Farewell! [*He dies.*

ESMERALDA.

Phœbus! He dies! In an instant everything is changed!

[*She falls upon his body.*

I follow you into eternity.

CLAUDE FROLLO.

Fatality!

THE PEOPLE.

Fatality!